To my Mum and Dad: who first put a pencil in my hand and encouraged me to copy those squiggly lines, kick-started my imagination with bedtime stories and audiobooks, and listened to me talk about wanting to be published until I found the confidence to just get on with it. Thank you.

Sent by God; foreseen by the prophets; descended from Kings and outcasts; preceded by John the Baptist. Born to a young, unmarried woman with an ordinary husband-to-be; at an unexpected time in an unlikely place.

Welcomed by the ordinary, the forgotten and the foreigner; feared by the powerful; forced into exile.

God incarnate.

CONTENTS

INTRODUCTION

It seems to me that there are two types of people when it comes to opening Christmas presents. There are those who throw themselves straight at them. No time to waste. Wrapping paper everywhere. One gift out then on to the next. Then there are those who take their time, savour the moment, enjoy that sense of expectancy. Maybe they even spread the opening of the presents over several days in order to make the experience last.

In the context of unwrapping presents that's a case of 'each to their own!' but during Advent we're called to take things slowly; knowing, hoping, believing that something wonderful is coming. Why, then, does Advent seem to disappear in a flurry of activity? The mission, it seems, is to ensure Christmas Day goes off without a hitch. Everything must be perfect: the presents, the food, the itinerary, the carols sung at the candle-lit service on Christmas Eve. Everything. Then, of course, there's the sense of anticlimax following 'the big day'? The Twelve Days of Christmas which take us to Epiphany lie forgotten underneath a pile of wrapping paper.

The events leading up to the first Christmas were far from the idyl of harmony and perfection we attempt to create at home and in church. It was a deeply human event; a glorious mess of possibility, danger and vulnerability. Jesus' early life sees him made known to Jews and foreigners, the faithful and the wicked; be presented to God at the Temple, only to become a refugee, fleeing from the devastation wreaked by one jealous man with far too much power.

If we choose, we can make links with today's world that are astonishing, exciting and sometimes heartbreaking.

This rather unassuming photo shows the sun shining through a high window of the Church of the Nativity in Bethlehem, the traditional birthplace of Jesus. Above the clamour and the tourists and the singing was this quiet reminder of why people have gathered there for centuries. At the entrance all sorts of people lay aside the things that divide them – and hopefully forget to pick them up when they leave – to focus on the coming of Jesus, the light shining through the darkness of troubled times.

So I invite you to grab a bible, hunker down in the season and make time to enter into the story. Beginning on 1st December and lasting to 6th January, each day will bring a short reflection on a relevant bible passage. The page facing provides an image and a few words to spark thought, providing an 'at a glance' option for days when you're caught up in the busyness of life.

Above all I hope this booklet helps you connect (or reconnect) with God in a way that brings you peace and hope; and that it provides just enough of a challenge to keep life interesting as you continue your travels with God.

Deacon Laura Evans

1ST DECEMBER
Read John 1: 1-14

John's gospel is the odd one out among the four accounts of Jesus' life and ministry.

Matthew and Luke start with their own reports of the events in Nazareth and Bethlehem; and while Mark skips over these early days, choosing to focus on the ministry of John the Baptist and Jesus' baptism, his gospel has a similar format and feel. 'This is what happened' they seem to say. Stories inevitably change with time and according to who's telling them so their accounts vary.

John's gospel is different. Rather than telling us what happened John shouts 'Look! This is why it matters!'

Sometimes, especially coming up to Christmas, we feel under pressure to appear excited and happy even when times are dark. At such times we tell people we are 'fine', then swiftly change the subject. Though this can be a joyful time full of love and laughter, recalling those people whose chairs are now empty or remembering the events of past Christmases can be painful.

John takes us all the way back to before creation, showing us who Jesus was and is: God making his home with us, present in the light and darkness of our own lives. He doesn't tell us,' The light shines in the darkness and makes everything bright,' but simply reminds us that the light of Jesus cannot be overwhelmed by darkness. The light of Jesus still burns brightly in our lives even, and perhaps most especially, when all we can see is darkness.

Whether you spend your Advent waiting in excitement, trepidation, delight, sorrow or a mixture of them all; I wish you light and life.

'The light shines in
the darkness, and the darkness
did not overcome it.'

At times it can be difficult to find the light.
Remember: even candles will splutter and die, but
the light of God never goes out.

2ND DECEMBER
Read Isaiah 9: 2, 6-7

Peace.

What is the first thing you think of when you hear that word?

'We're travelling 400 miles in 3 days.'
'I'm cooking for 16 on Christmas Day - dreading it.'
'I always miss ….. at Christmas.'
I'll be on my own this year.'
'I haven't done any shopping yet. Avoiding it for as long as I can!'
'It's costing a fortune. Not sure how we'll manage.'
'It's the most stressful time of year.'
'I wish it was over!'

These are just a few comments I've overheard recently on buses, in the streets and in the supermarket. Maybe you can empathise.

For many people the celebration of the birth of the Prince of Peace has become a time of stress and pressure and the truth is most if not all of us experience some or all of these feelings at Christmastime. It's a time of complex and varying emotions and the Advent and Christmas seasons can feel overwhelming. It's perfectly normal to feel concerned about the logistics of visiting a wide-spread family, feel lonely or alone, worry about catering quandaries, want to get people lovely presents or to miss loved ones.

Jesus is not separate from the festivities but can be found within them; bringing a peace quite different from anything the world can give.

How might you weave that sense of peace into your celebrations?

Where will you
find

Peace

today?

3RD DECEMBER
Read Micah 5: 2

Bethlehem is, unsurprisingly, forever associated with Christmas; but it does appear elsewhere in the bible.

It features even as far back as Genesis where it is near to the burial place of Jacob's wife, Rachel. Bethlehem is also the home Naomi, her husband and sons flee during a famine; and to which Naomi returns as a widow, with only her foreign daughter-in-law Ruth for company. Ruth, of course, shows herself to be love and loyalty personified and eventually becomes the great grandmother of David, King of Israel.

> Rachel was unable to have children for many years and was derided by her sister.

> Naomi suffered the shame of returning to her homeland having lost all that she once had.

> Ruth was a Moabite; entirely 'other'. Not respectable company.

> David, the youngest son, is originally left behind to mind the sheep when Samuel comes to anoint one of Jesse's sons. He is the least likely candidate for kingship.

> Ruth and David are among Jesus' ancestors.

Even at birth, the Son of God can be found against a backdrop of the powerless and the undervalued; those written-off by society. He may be distantly descended from kings but he is also the child of outcasts and strangers.

Where do you look for Jesus?

Would you expect to find him among people like these?

Do you look for God in unlikely places?

4TH DECEMBER
Read Isaiah 11: 1-5

Christianity has a reputation for judgement. There have been times when we have taken it upon ourselves to decide who is (and isn't) welcome at the table; or focused on hell, fire and damnation preaching rather than speaking of the love of God; or punished any we perceive not to live up to our moral standards without pausing to consider their circumstances.

These accusations of hypocrisy are not always undeserved.

Is it surprising, then, that many people imagine anger to be God's default emotion; supposing God goes around picking faults and looking for reasons to condemn us? While it is wonderful that today so many Christian communities are diverse and welcoming, isn't it a pity this cannot be assumed and taken as the norm?

This passage from Isaiah speaks of one who will not judge by what he sees and hears but shows wisdom, understanding and righteousness. John's gospel records how, eight-hundred-years later, a carpenter from Nazareth defended a woman caught in adultery, reminding those who sought to condemn her of their own unworthiness and failings.

This is what Jesus did: reminded us that we are not the ones who get to make the decisions about who is worthy of God's love and God's forgiveness. We are simply not that powerful. That is God's job. Where we see 'wrong', God sees the whole story.

It may make us uncomfortable; understanding that God shows wisdom and faithfulness to those we'd rather not be seen with or have as part of our community. Jesus never said it would be easy. Only that he would be there to make the journey with us.

If you ever feel foolish, or frightened, or a failure, remember our God is faithful and wise.

God knows us through and through.

5TH DECEMBER
Read Isaiah 11: 6-9

This is all very well if you're the wolf. Not so good if you're the lamb.

If you're the wolf you know your intentions are honourable. You're not going to eat your new friend. You just want to spend time embracing your new-found vegetarianism and getting to know the neighbours. You may not understand why the lamb keeps pushing you away. Why is it so stand-offish?

If you're the lamb you're going to be on your guard; presupposing you haven't already run off very fast in the opposite direction. How long would it take for you to trust this huge animal? It may say it means you no harm, but you've seen teeth and claws like that before, and it's never ended well.

Who are the people with power in your community or country? How do they respond to the needs of those less able to care for themselves? Can they be trusted?

Who is vulnerable, frightened or at risk? How might their experiences have shaped their ability to recognise and accept genuine kindness?

It is only by being fully present to one another that we can even begin to answer any of these questions. If we continue to divide humanity, talking about groups of people as 'other' and only associate with those we think are 'like us', we cannot achieve the level of trust Isaiah foresees as part of God's Kingdom.

Lest we forget, Jesus showed infinite love and patience to people no-one else wanted to touch; the only people ever to make him angry were those who abused their power.

What does it mean to trust another person?

What does it mean to trust God?

6TH DECEMBER
Read Matthew 1: 1-17

It will probably shock no-one that the first 17 verses of Matthew's gospel are very rarely read in church! There is a certain sinking feeling which can only be experienced by those who agree to read from scripture at the last minute only to discover long, unfamiliar words filing across the page. My heart goes out to anyone who has ever faced a genealogy of Jesus in these circumstances!

There are two accounts of Jesus' ancestry in the gospels, the other is in Luke 3. They are not the same, and the question of why this is has haunted theologians for centuries. Interesting though is a different question: why are these lists of names there in the first place?! What possible interest could they hold?

There are names here that many of us will recognise, not always for positive reasons: Judah mistook his daughter-in-law for a prostitute and through her became the father of Perez, from whom Jesus is descended; David himself behaves badly, abusing his power in order to murder Uriah after sleeping with his wife.

If Jesus had been born into a fictional, perfect, wholesome family how would any of us relate to him? We know that human beings are a diverse bunch - flawed and wonderful, fallible and kind - and God knows that too. Thus we find Matthew's account of Jesus' story beginning with a list of names: the 'sinner' recorded among the 'righteous', the rich-and-powerful and the poor-and-forgotten listed together as equals.

Then all these people go into the great mixing pot, God jumps in and Jesus, who can be equally claimed by everyone, makes sure nothing is ever the same again. Thank God!

Do you see a cross-section of humanity here
or just a list of names?

Do you take time to get to know the people
behind the names you read in your everyday
life?

7TH DECEMBER
Read Matthew 1: 1-17

What? Again? Surely we had enough of that list of names yesterday. Bear with me!

There is something phenomenal about this genealogy. Something profoundly unusual setting it apart from virtually every similar list not just in scripture but in ancient history: but what is it?

Women. Very few women are named in the Old Testament. When we see a female mentioned we can be sure of a powerful story.

If you wish, have a look at some or all of the following:
    Tamar's story in Genesis 38
    Rahab's story in Joshua 2
    Ruth's story in the book of Ruth
    The wife of Uriah's story in 2 Samuel 11-12

Examining the events of these times means acknowledging an uncomfortable truth that for centuries women were mere possessions to be passed from father to husband to son. Each of these women was incredibly vulnerable without this protecting male figure.

The males found their place in this list by right. Women must earn it through monumental bravery, great grief and struggle, unbelievable cunning or lifelong loyalty. Most of Jesus' female ancestors go unrecalled. They were unimportant - not worthy of a name.

Without them this, or any other, family tree could not exist.

Today, remember people whose names and stories are at risk of being forgotten and lost. If you can, listen to them.

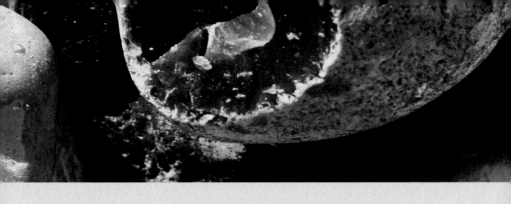

Who are the brave women in your life?

8TH DECEMBER
Read Isaiah 40: 3-5

God uses the lips of Isaiah to conjure up some profoundly evocative images, including this one. It's so powerful that it is quoted as a prologue to Mark's gospel.

Plainly John is an important figure in the life and ministry of Jesus, even though he plays a small part in the events of the gospels. Once Jesus' ministry is established, John slips into the background and we hear little more of him except the account of his death.

John finds himself in an 'in between' place. On one side he has the prophets of old, on the other he has Jesus on the cusp of his ministry. John must look back at what has been, point forward towards the future, and, with God's help, somehow reconcile the two. To add insult to injury John will not see the journey of Jesus ministry, experience the terror of the crucifixion or know the joy of resurrection. His task is to be instrumental to its beginning.

Playing a supporting role can be hard, especially when we do not get to see what happens next. It is human nature to want credit and praise for our actions, and Christians are not immune to that.

We may accompany a person or group for a season; helping them navigate through a transitional period of their own lives, only to be forgotten in the flurry of whatever happens next. Spend some time thinking about those for whom you have helped 'prepare the way', including those whose lives you have impacted without knowing it.

We may also forget to credit those who came before us, whose prayers and hard work crafted the foundations on which we build.

Take a moment to recall them and thank God for them.

Who has guided you in faith?
How might you guide others?

9TH DECEMBER
Read Malachi 4: 5-6

Malachi is believed to be the last of the Old Testament prophets. These words, written in about 400BC foretell the coming of another Elijah - one who will point out God's ways and turn God's people to one another. 'Just wait,' says Malachi. 'He's coming.'

And after that? Silence. Nothing. God seems to close the shop, lock the doors and walk away. The prophecies are learned and recited but very few pay attention or consider what they might mean. It's all a dim memory of something that happened in another time, another place.

It's tempting to take a convenient jump from the prophets to the familiar New Testament stories, ignoring the silence in favour of the action. The idea of God being silent or keeping us waiting is disconcerting and not something we want to dwell on. We want clear signs, easy answers and comfortable half truths.

Yet we know that God was still working on the tapestry of life throughout those four-hundred years; waiting for the right time to change the pattern of creation. God never forgot the prophecies or lost sight of the people.

If we read scripture chronologically the next thing to happen is recorded in Mark: suddenly and dramatically John the Baptist bursts forth from the wilderness, catching people by surprise. He's not the Messiah - he's the one who goes before him proclaiming the glorious truth: It's happening! God is making home among us!

We wait for that voice in the wilderness of our own lives, and give thanks for the patient commitment of those who came before us.

Four-hundred years of silence, but the light of God did not go out.

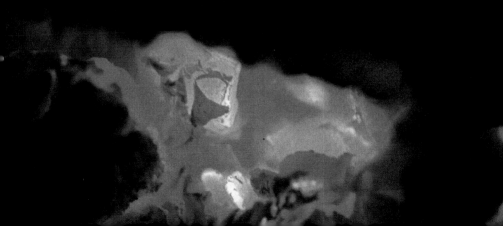

10TH DECEMBER
Read Luke 1: 5-25

I feel sorry for Zechariah. We may know that through God anything is possible, but how often do we create God in our own image, forgetting that God breaks down barriers and flattens boundaries.

Zechariah says he and Elizabeth are 'old'. How old is 'old'? Who knows? Old enough to have given up hope of conceiving a longed for child. Old enough for Elizabeth to feel the scorn of the neighbours for having failed in her 'duty' as a wife. Old enough for Zechariah to express uncertainty even when faced with an angel from God. His family doesn't conform to expectations. How could that ever change?

Family life can be incredibly complicated at the best of times, and for many Christmas brings it all into sharp focus. Bombarded as we are by images of the perfect family, many may feel like outsiders, especially if our family relationships don't conform to the assumptions of others.

Not all stories end like Elizabeth and Zechariah's. Family life for many is not what they hoped for, or what others expect. There are:

Those who will be asked intrusive questions about their childlessness over Christmas dinner.

Those trying to pretend everything is normal as they grieve a child.

Those who are unwelcome at their family gatherings or for whom 'family' conjures up difficult memories.

Maybe our lesson here is that we need to be the miracle: to travel alongside those who don't conform to our expectations rather than asking why they aren't more like us?

Have you ever been slow
to believe God will
answer your prayers?

11TH DECEMBER
Read Luke 1: 39-45

The baby in Elizabeth's womb jumps for joy at the sight of Mary. Even before his birth John knows that he is in the presence of the Lord. Not until she feels him leap inside her does Elizabeth makes the connection and rejoice that Mary has been blessed and is carrying a child who will be an even greater blessing.

Elizabeth's experience was one of a kind, but she is not alone in having the Holy Spirit speak to her through a child. There is something truly beautiful about allowing a young child to point out the way along the path of faith and bring us to a greater understanding of God.

What could we learn about God's love if we took a pause from the trials and tribulations of adulthood to watch a little one rejoice in a gloriously imperfect sandcastle?

How would we treat God's creation if we joined the muddy five-year-old in marvelling at the range of life existing under a stone?

What difference would it make to our relationships if we took the attitude of the baby in the pushchair who squirms with delight at the sight of someone they know and love?

This is life before the expectations of the world kick in and squash our joy, creativity and curiosity into the deep recesses of our memories in an attempt to appear 'grown-up'. After a while we can cease to remember the importance of these things.

It is then that we need children to remind, teach and guide us.

John leapt for joy in his mother's womb. When was the last time your heart leapt for joy? Can you bring that joy to others this Christmas?

What can we learn from listening more deeply to children?

12TH DECEMBER
Read Luke 1: 26-38

We're now entering the realm of the comfy, cosy Christmas story; the stuff of school plays and the much-loved Christmas carols that have played for months already in shops.

There's nothing wrong with those things of course; they help people who would not normally engage with scripture to do so in a positive way and can sow seeds that others will nurture. That said, there comes a time in our journey of faith when we need to put aside the immaculate costume replete with blue headdress. This is not a chocolate-box story but the life of a real human being.

Lukes matter-of-fact account of the annunciation belies the amazing chain of events that are unfolding here. The appearance of an angel and news of a child to be conceived by the Holy Spirit is not an everyday affair - the fate of humanity rests on this moment. Mary's own life will never be the same and she must have known the risk she was taking in saying 'yes' to God.

Mary's story can make us feel inadequate. What would we do if confronted with Mary's decision?

Is it helpful, though, to think like that? Mary's willingness to answer God's call was an act of phenomenal bravery that changed the course of the future. But this is Mary's story, not ours. Rather than beating ourselves up about stepping into Mary's sandals we need to be grounded in a different question: What is God's will for me in the here and now? After all, we were created to be unique, not imitations.

Today, think about how you can be a one-of-a-kind example; saying 'yes' to God's call.

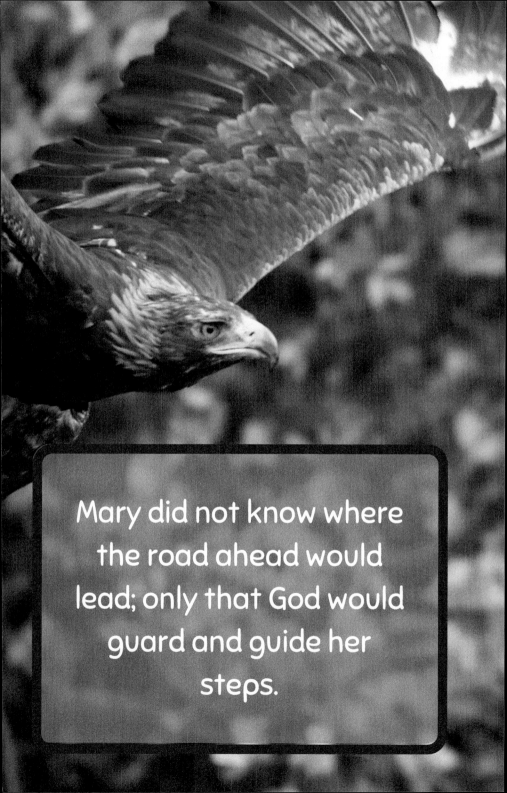

Mary did not know where the road ahead would lead; only that God would guard and guide her steps.

13TH DECEMBER
Read Luke 1: 26-38

I wonder how Mary felt when the angel had gone. Luke tells us she was troubled when the angel greeted her – that's hardly a surprise – but he leaves out any detail of what happened afterwards. She agreed to be part of this extraordinary miracle and surrendered herself to God, but that doesn't mean Mary felt entirely comfortable and at peace with the situation. After all, this is not some inaccessible figure, or a picture on a Christmas card, but a young woman facing an unforeseen fork in the road of her own future.

How did Mary feel when her monthly cycle stopped and the pregnancy went from a promise to a reality? Remember those who gaze at a positive test and scarcely believe their eyes. Those who have longed for this day and now face yet more waiting and hoping.

Did Mary try to hide her changing body? Remember those who are not ready to share their news, or are uncertain of their own feelings.

What did Mary's mother and father say? Remember those who experience silence, rejection or homelessness due to pregnancy, and those whose families want to be supportive but don't know how.

Did Mary tell Joseph herself, or did he find out some other way? Remember those who fear sharing the news with a partner. Those who are abused, vulnerable or uncertain of the reaction.

Faced with exclusion and perhaps worse, did Mary ever wish this was happening to someone else? Remember those whose pregnancies place them at risk, those for whom fear outweighs rejoicing.

When you remember Mary, remember them.

Light a candle in your heart for anyone who is frightened today.

14TH DECEMBER
Read Luke 1: 46-56

The words of 'The Magnificat', are spoken during Mary's visit to Elizabeth. Mary is an unlikely character in the unfolding story, yet her song of the redemption, blessings and mercy to be found in God's topsy-turvey Kingdom is still heard in churches across the world.

Luke's gospel records Mary as staying with Elizabeth for three months. Maybe she went to help her cousin prepare for the coming child; or was she sent away to her supportive older relative to hide the pregnancy? Either way, though Mary's rejoicing contrasts sharply with her precarious situation she is still able to call herself 'blessed' and honour God for all God has done.

Mary's life will not become easier after Jesus' birth. Soon she'll have to watch her son ask uncomfortable questions, challenge the authorities and surround himself with down-and-outs. One day she'll kneel at the foot of the cross and watch her precious boy, of whom so much had been expected, die a criminal's death.

I wonder if she wept, recalling the day she and Elizabeth rejoiced in God's goodness; or if she laughed without humour at the very idea she could think herself 'blessed'.

We could hardly blame Mary if she did feel that way. Yet the blessing doesn't come through a chain of events and experiences, but from God. 'The Lord is with you,' says the angel in Luke 1: 28. Nothing can make Mary 'less blessed' because God is with her in the darkness of Calvary just as God is there in the shining light of resurrection.

Mary's son will one day teach his followers the Beatitudes (Matthew 5: 1-12). How do these compare to Mary's situation?

Do you feel
Blessed?

What does that
word mean to you?

15TH DECEMBER
Read Matthew 1: 18-19

Joseph. We know little about him and even less about his relationship with Mary. They both lived in Nazareth so we can assume they knew each other, and they would have met at the betrothal ceremony, but it was probably an arranged marriage.

It's difficult for us to comprehend the situation Matthew describes in a few sentences. Betrothal was as legally binding as marriage. Joseph knows he's not the father so the baby was conceived in adultery; the punishment for which is stoning. He may well be under pressure from friends, family and religious leaders to make an example of Mary; to show what happens to unchaste women. News travels fast in small communities, staying in Nazareth exposes mother and child to danger.

Countless women have stood in Mary's shoes. Killed, threatened or reviled for being pregnant outside marriage; forced to make devastating decisions or having those decisions made for them. In quietly releasing her from the betrothal Joseph gives Mary an opportunity to leave the area (perhaps go to her cousin, Elizabeth), think up a story to cover her 'shame' or come home at a later date without the baby. Seemingly there can be no happy ending, but Joseph chooses what he percieves to be the safest option for her and the baby.

Many of us are in the habit of telling ourselves we have no power. This comforting fiction absolves us of responsibility, placing it firmly on the shoulders of those we perceive to be more important. We may rarely have the power of life or death but we choose how to use our resources; welcoming the person no-one else 'sees' is a monumental use of power.

What power do you have over others?

Do you seek to do what is right?

Can you admit when you're wrong?

16TH DECEMBER
Read Matthew 1: 20-25

If we look at the past without rose-tinted glasses we see an uncomfortable truth: family life has always been complicated. Historically the illusion of a nuclear family was seen as something to be preserved at all costs, and before the days of DNA and social media uncomfortable truths were not always discussed. Hopefully, we are now beginning to realise the full spectrum and glorious technicolour of family life, and that the nuclear family, though a wonderful thing for many, is not the only place to raise a family.

In marrying Mary, Joseph takes on full responsibility for the coming child. Joseph will find a safe place for Mary to give birth and listen to God's instruction to take mother and baby to Egypt. He'll join the panic when the twelve-year-old Jesus cannot be found on the road home from Jerusalem and later teach him a carpenters' trade. In short, Joseph will provide for Jesus, protect him from those who would do him harm, worry about him and invest in his future. They may not share blood but Joseph is a true parent to the young Jesus.

Do you know someone who has stepped into the role of parent in a similar way? You certainly will, even if you're not aware of the situation. Perhaps that person is you.

Remembering the importance of good, supportive role-models, give thanks for those who raise and care for children, especially:

Anyone who has been told that theirs is not a 'proper family' because it does not meet someone else's criteria; or that they are not a 'real parent' because they do not share blood-links with their child.

Those who raise grandchildren or other young relatives.

The angel's words offer a chink of light in the darkness.

A new family is forming.

17TH DECEMBER
Read Luke 2: 1-3

One would have thought Mary and Joseph had quite enough going on without having to make an unexpected seventy-mile journey to Bethlehem!

Imagine Joseph's heart sinking when he realises there's nothing for it, they have to go. He doesn't know where they will stay or how he'll ensure the safety of Mary and the baby.

Imagine Mary's anxiety as she faces giving birth to her first child far from home and without a female relative by her side.

Imagine them gazing at their possessions and wondering what to take. They don't know how long they'll be away. Will anything left behind still be there when they return? Will they return?

Remember those for whom this is lived experience even today.

Forced from their homes due to natural disaster or crop failure or living with the uncertainty and danger of war.

Hounded out by corrupt governments or fleeing persecution.

Fleeing domestic abuse.

Arriving home to find an eviction notice on the door.

Jesus was born under a borrowed roof, to a mother far from home. What if we saw him in the eyes of every vulnerable person?

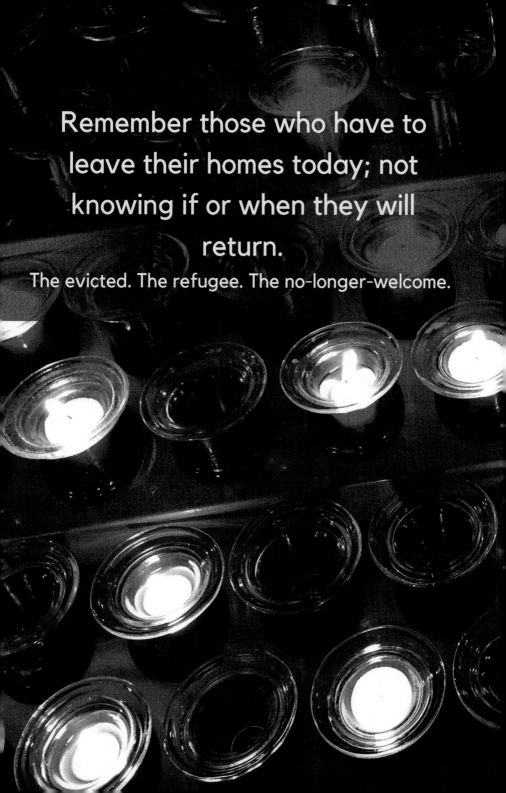

Remember those who have to leave their homes today; not knowing if or when they will return.

The evicted. The refugee. The no-longer-welcome.

18TH DECEMBER
Read Luke 2: 4-5

Poor Mary. In the late stages of pregnancy with each step taking her further from home the journey must have been awful.

For a moment allow yourself to enter the scene on the road from Nazareth to Bethlehem.

What can you see? Did they have a donkey? Maybe even a little cart? Maybe they were able to get lifts with friends or strangers. Possibly they even travelled some of the way with neighbours who were off to other towns and cities. What did Mary think about as she bounced uncomfortably along?

What can you hear? It must have been noisy on the road. So many people going hither and thither. Was Mary able to take a nap, or does she long for the peace and quiet of home? Did she talk to anyone?Personally, I like to think that among the thousands of people on the roads there was at least one kind older woman who took pity on a young mother-to-be; walking or riding with her for a while and helping prepare her for what lay ahead. Angels come in many different forms.

What do you feel? What is the atmosphere on the road? Are people excited; looking forward to meeting relatives or greeting friends? Are they irritated at having to make the journey? Do they share their food and shelter or keep it to themselves? Where do they sleep?

It can be helpful to step into scripture like this. It reminds us of the humanity behind these cosy, comfy tales. As you travel through the rest of Advent try to spend some time reflecting on the daily passage either as an observer, or by putting yourself in the place of one of the people who were there.

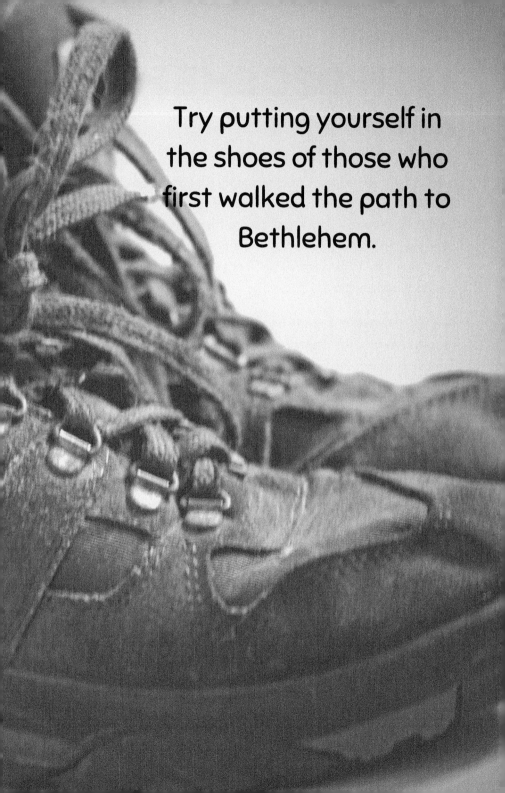

Try putting yourself in the shoes of those who first walked the path to Bethlehem.

19TH DECEMBER
Read Luke 2: 4-5

There's an 'elephant in the room' here. From an early age we're taught a version of the Christmas story that combines bits of Matthew and Luke with some educated guesses and a few fanciful additions. We know that Mary gave birth among the animals because there was no room at the inn. We've probably heard at least one little 'innkeeper' shout 'There's no room!' with gusto during a school nativity play!

Why did they need to worry at all about where they would stay? The reason they're in Bethlehem is that Joseph is distantly descended from King David. Presumably all his male relatives have had to decamp there. It's not beyond the realms of possibility that he has relatives or friends living in the city. Why is no-one offering to put them up, or offering them their guest room? After all, Mary's about to give birth!

I may be reading too much into this, but the circumstances of Mary's pregnancy are known to be... odd. Joseph isn't the father and he seems to have fallen for some story about Mary carrying God's child. News like this travels fast and you can almost hear the scoffing.

There is no mention of any female relative, or indeed anyone at all, being present at Jesus' birth. Instead, Mary and Joseph are alone and Jesus' first visitors won't be adoring grandparents or even delighted friends but strangers.

Throughout the world there are parents like Mary and Joseph; having to cope without the support of family because of estrangement, death or physical distance. Bring them to mind.

God travelled with Mary and Joseph,
even when they seemed utterly alone.

God travels with you, too.

20TH DECEMBER
Think about The Inn

Before we try to understand the circumstances of Jesus' birth we must first put aside all our modern assumptions and expectations about inns, guest rooms and other forms of accommodation for travellers.

Something recognisable as an 'inn' did exist at the time of Jesus' birth. These were essentially large courtyards and largely reserved for merchants, wanderers and the associated animals. A place such as this would not have been an option for the pregnant Mary. It's much more likely that it was the 'lodging houses', spare rooms attached to a family home, that were full and closed to them.

Scripture tells us that Jesus was lain in a manger, and modern readers thus assume him to have been born in a stable. It was common in first century Palestine for animals to share living space with their owners; livestock sleeping downstairs and humans upstairs if room allowed. Chances are Mary gave birth in the family room of an ordinary private home. A space as clean as was practically possible, warmed by the animals with whom the family shared their lives. Whose home is a mystery.

In many ways Jesus came into the world in the same circumstances as most of his peers, in an ordinary house among ordinary people. Yet, unlike most others, he is dependent on the kindness and hospitality of strangers.

I wonder if the owners of that house knew who the baby grew up to be? I wonder if they followed his progress? What do you think?

In first century Palestine humans and animals lived under the same roof, each relying on the other for protection and care.

Can you create more safe spaces for the living things surrounding you?

21ST DECEMBER
Think about The Angels

Scripture is teeming with angels. Combining Matthew and Luke's accounts of the circumstances leading up to Jesus' birth we see Zechariah, Mary and Joseph all experience some form of visitation. To say nothing of the shepherds, magi and others whose encounters happen soon after, and those like Elizabeth who are directly affected by news from a messenger they do not meet face-to-face.

Yet they are by no means the first in scripture to encounter an angel. That accolade probably belongs to Abraham, Jesus' ancestor whose experience is chronicled in Genesis 18. Sitting outside his tent in the heat of the day Abraham notices three strangers standing before him. Jewish law compels him to provide a little food and water to sustain them, but, in an act of sacrificial hospitality, Abraham runs about ensuring a generous welcome and an ample feast. In the words of Hebrews 13:2 Abraham 'entertained angels without knowing it' and, as is so often the way, his life would never be the same.

There are many beliefs and traditions surrounding angels which take us beyond the white, lacy, tinsel-bedecked characters of the traditional nativity play. The Greek word 'angelos' bears no resemblance to this image, translating into modern English as 'messenger'. It is used several hundred times in scripture to refer to human as well heavenly individuals.

With this in mind, have you ever met an angel, or experienced an encounter so spiritually charged that you believed yourself to be in the presence of the divine? Are there times when you might entertain angels without knowing it, and how can you show radical hospitality there? Reading about such visitations is one thing, recognising God's messengers is quite another.

Angels.
Messengers.
Dreams.

How does God speak to you?

How do you speak to God?

Are you willing to listen?

22ND DECEMBER
Think about The Shepherds

What? You might be thinking that, like over-eager actors, the shepherds have somehow wandered on stage far too early. After all, they're not in this scene, are they? Their part comes right at the very end of the nativity - after the birth of Jesus.

You'd be right. Their time hasn't yet come. Today they're engaged in their ancient occupation; one shared with more than a few key figures in the Old Testament. In the intervening centuries public opinion has changed. What was once seen as a respectable job is no longer so highly regarded. Yes, like so many they're awaiting the Messiah, but they can hardly expect him to come in their lifetime, or to them personally; so they're just working and living their lives.

Sitting on the hill among the sheep they tend, these shepherds cannot know that within days they'll be visited by angels and invited to be among the first to kneel in the presence of the Messiah. Soon they'll be the first evangelists, sharing the good news as they sell milk and wool in the town, or offer lambs for sacrifice at the Temple. Right now they are ordinary shepherds and today is an ordinary day.

Luke's gospel disregards their backstory. We don't buy an autobiography for accounts of average work days, but for the bits that make the person interesting. Many of us would skim those parts even if they were ever written down.

Some may take this attitude in their lives: avoiding those people, jobs or activities they perceive as mundane. If you ever catch yourself doing that, think about these 'average' shepherds. They were the first to hear the news. The first to be caught up in a series of events that changed the world. Today: look for God in the ordinary.

23RD DECEMBER
Think about Joseph

There's a baby coming. This is starting to feel uncomfortably real.

We know so little about Joseph; we can't be sure this was his first experience of parenthood. It's not beyond the realms of possibility that he'd been married before and already had children.

I wonder how he felt watching Mary's body grow and change.

Excited? This new life has so much potential after all. Mary is hours away from giving birth to a child foreseen by angels. A child conceived, not in the normal way, but by the seed of the Holy Spirit. What if that's only the beginning of a huge adventure?

Anxious? This child isn't his. Joseph swore to give him a name and a home. He's prepared to love and accept the child but what if, when he looks at the baby, he feels nothing but resentment?

Scared? At this time mothers died in childbirth with terrifying regularity; babies too. Joseph may have signed up for all this when he chose to remain at Mary's side rather than divorce her but what if it all goes wrong? What if...? No, best not think about that.

Joseph is probably experiencing a whole spectrum of emotions simultaneously. We know he's a good man; that he does the right thing. Yet right now there's nothing he can do except try to keep his mind under control. The weight of the world on his shoulders; past words and actions flickering through his mind.

Joseph's situation is one-of-a-kind but he is not the only person to ever experience a lack of control; to have nothing to do but watch, wait, hope and pray. Pray for those who know that feeling.

Remember those
who can do nothing
but watch and pray
tonight.

CHRISTMAS EVE
Think about Mary

There's a baby coming. All this is starting to feel uncomfortably real.

Imagine Mary squirming, trying to get comfortable as she attempts to sleep the night away. The baby inside her moves too, his tiny hands and feet causing her stomach to expand and release. It's nearly time.

Imagine Mary pulling herself out of the makeshift bed prepared for her. Without any real purpose she moves about the room, running her fingers over the coats of the animals whose space she shares. Yes, there's plenty of clean water in the pitcher, enough cosy straw in the manger. True, it's not where and how she imagined giving birth to her first child; but it's much better than nothing.

Imagine Mary placing her hand on her widening stomach. He's moving more than usual tonight. Older women have smiled, saying hers will be a big, healthy baby. They don't know what she knows. He'll be more than they could even comprehend. Her mind flashes to the future. This special child; what will he be like? What will it mean to be a mother; his mother? It won't be long before she finds out.

Imagine Mary wincing. More than backache and exhaustion she's starting to feel pain. Not all the time. Not bad enough to wake Joseph and the others. Is that normal? Her mind forms a list of unforeseen questions. How much does it hurt? Will she know if something is going wrong? How long will it all take?

Imagine Mary jerking forward suddenly, her hands pressing into the wall. She tries to stifle the growing panic as her body prepares itself for the birth. Stay calm. There's a long way to go yet. Joseph stirs, then wakes. Their eyes meet in the darkness. It's time.

Pray for those who are
sleepless tonight.

Those who are anxious.
Those who are working.
Those who are in pain.
Those kept awake by the needs of others.

CHRISTMAS DAY

Read Luke 2: 4-7

There's a baby in the manger.
God and child. Divine and human.
Foreseen yet somehow unexpected.
Heaven reveals itself on earth.

Child. Dependent, small and vulnerable.
Relying on others for protection and care.
Yet not in robes of gold or purple,
or in a cradle rocked by slaves.

God. Divine, older than the universe.
Creation's light shines from his face.
Yet swaddled in what lay to hand.
Sleeping under a borrowed roof.

Crackling with pure potential,
And so a new chapter of history begins.
Soon a teacher. Rabbi. Saviour.
Torchlight-bearer in a dark-filled world.

Breathing God-breath on flickering flames.
Igniting a blaze of love and justice.
Burning through boundaries.
Binding the broken. Brightening lives.

Though, for now a tiny baby.
Those that truly look will see,
The light of God that shines behind
Those ancient, newborn, sparkling eyes.

Jesus Christ,
Incarnate God.
Breathe your God-breath on me.
Fan my flickering faith into
flames that can be passed
on to others.
Amen

BOXING DAY
Read Luke 2: 8-15

The theme of shepherds and sheep is woven through scripture from Abel, son of Adam and Eve onwards. Who can forget the promises of Psalm 23; or David being called in from the fields to be anointed King of Israel? How fitting that these should be the first visitors to the cradle of God.

In first century Palestine the image of the shepherds on the hillside carefully tending their sheep would have been familiar and comfortable. At that time the sheep would follow the shepherd wherever he went, relying on his protection from predators. He would find them the best grass and knew where to shelter from the weather. The shepherd was entirely responsible for their welfare.

Jesus is the epitome of the perfect shepherd; but surely this ancient metaphor is no longer culturally relevant today. Too much has changed in the world of sheep and shepherding, right? Wrong.

Jesus would never have included a sheepdog in his stories or parables. They had never been used in that area to herd sheep. Yet contemporary shepherds are rarely seen without an animal at their side. The dog might not always know the overall purpose, but they've learned to recognise the call of the shepherd and respond accordingly. Anyone who has ever owned a dog will know the training never ends!

How would our faith life be different if we understood that we were always in training, with new things to learn and old skills to sharpen?

Could you be both sheep and sheepdog?

Who do you watch over in prayer?

27TH DECEMBER
Read Luke 2: 16-20

It was early morning when the shepherds left. The animals, having been thoroughly disturbed by an eventful night, are slow to rouse themselves long enough to investigate the contents of their manger. Just as well. The baby is quiet - for now at least.

Mary is still exhausted by childbirth and all that has happened since. She lies half asleep in the hay, her head finding the comfortable spot on Joseph's bony shoulder. So much has changed since she had her own experience of angels that day in Nazareth. Back then all this had been a daunting prospect - equal parts exciting and terrifying. She would have a son. He would be the Messiah.

And now there he was.

One of the shepherds had stroked Jesus' palm. The baby's fist curled around the rough, calloused finger, attaching himself firmly to his new friend. Mary had seen tears on the cheeks of the unassuming man and he'd not attempted to escape the infant's grip; choosing to crouch in silence by the manger as his friends spoke of angels, music and light in the sky. When the time came for them to leave each shepherd bowed to the baby, but he lifted her son's hand and bestowed upon it a kiss as tender as any mother's. As he got to his feet their eyes met and he smiled as if he'd only just remembered how.

Her son, not even a day old and already softening hearts.

Her son. The Messiah. Carrying him in her womb was one thing. Watching over him as he grew would be quite another. More exciting? Probably. More terrifying? Certainly. She murmured a prayer over him and lapsed into sleep.

How does the presence of Jesus affect your life?

28TH DECEMBER
Read Luke 2: 22-24

Jesus was born in a time and place steeped in religious tradition. Leviticus dicated that a woman should be considered 'unclean' for 40 days following the birth of a son, during which time she could not mix with the public. At the end of this time Leviticus 12 dictated she must present an offering at the Temple.

At the time of Jesus, and in the early years of the church, the focus of attention was on the mother. This isn't surprising – childbirth has never been a safe process and a lack of basic sanitation made it even more risky in those days. Our modern foreheads may wrinkle at the idea of a new mother being closeted at home for forty or eighty days, but this largely protected her and the baby from infections carried by others.

Think about how your own church acknowledges the birth of a child. Do you practice infant baptism? Is there a Dedication Service? If your church has a standard liturgy perhaps get hold of a copy and have a look at what is said and who is celebrated.

Christian tradition is as diverse as we might expect. The early church generally upheld the rules laid out in Leviticus, while the medieval period brought the concept of 'churching' the mother to give thanks for her surviving childbirth. This practice has largely died out in Britain since the Second Vatican Counsel, although liturgies are still available in older publications. Attitudes to infant baptism vary from culture to culture and often within denominations, although most have some custom for celebrating the birth or adoption of a child.

We can be tempted to consider 'our way' the best and most faithful to God's will. Instead let's be open to celebrating key life events in ways that are culturally relevant and affirming to all concerned.

Luke chose to edit Leviticus 12. A sacrifice of two pigeons or doves was appropriate only for those who could not afford to offer a lamb.

God's own son was redeemed for the same price as a poor family's child.

29TH DECEMBER
Read Luke 2: 25-35

Prompted by the Holy Spirit, Simeon hurries to the Temple and encounters Mary, Joseph and the infant Jesus.

How does Simeon react to seeing the baby? What does he say? How does he hold him? Is there laughter? Are there tears?

Simeon has lived a life of service to God. He is a truly righteous man and his entire life has built up to the moment when the child who will bring light and salvation is placed in his arms. It's no wonder Simeon was moved to speak the words many will now recognise as the Benedictus; the emotion must have been tangible.

He turns and offers a word of blessing over Mary and Joseph, but the mood has changed. For the first time Simeon is made aware of the magnitude of what it means to be the Messiah and the impact his life and ministry will have on those who love him most.

'A sword will pierce your own soul,' he says.

What does one say to that? It isn't surprising Luke doesn't record a response. Was Mary shocked by the words, or was she already beginning to understand the implications of being this child's mother?

Joseph generally stands forgotten in this, as in other scenes. Does he speak? What's his body language like? Who is he looking at?

Mary and Joseph's situation is unique; but they are not the only people to ever receive life-changing news about a child in their care. Give thanks with those who rejoice and pray for those who struggle.

Pray for those who are concerned about the health, welfare or future of children in their care.

30TH DECEMBER
Read Luke 2: 36-38

While the tale of Simeon's encounter with the Holy Family spans ten verses, Anna's is limited to just two. Yet these lines offer a moving account of a woman utterly devoted to the God she serves.

Anna could not have lived at the Temple. Only priests and Levites were accorded that honour. Luke implies she is a constant presence when the Temple was open for worship. She has no official capacity, no special role. The Temple leaders may not even have acknowledged her presence. She simply offers prayer and fasting to God.

Some might say that Anna was abdicating responsibility; retreating from the harsh realities of life. Anna has experienced her share of struggle. A short marriage; a long widowhood. Who can blame her if she retreats from society in order to live out the rest of her days in quiet, untroubled by the problems of the world.

I suspect the opposite. To my mind Anna is the grandmother of the Temple; her corner the first-century equivalent of the comfortable chair by the fire. A listening ear. A reliable, unshakable, constant presence. Those in need of prayer would have known exactly where to find her and would be totally assured of her promise to hold them before God. I wonder what quiet wisdom this godly woman imparted to those who came to her.

These people would surely have been captivated by tales of the infant Messiah. Luke throws it in as a casual comment, but Anna would be a familiar face amongst those who most longed for a change in regime.

People like Anna usually don't speak often, but when they do it's always a good idea to listen.

Who are
the 'Annas'
in your life
and
community?

NEW YEAR'S EVE
Read Matthew 2: 1-2

... and so we return to the familiar narrative of the season.

The magi enter stage left. Mary adjusts the 'baby' in her arms, the shepherds, angels, donkey, star, sheep and assorted other characters huddle together on the stage. Joseph stamps his foot and refuses to move closer to Mary.

It's tempting at this time of year to perform a 'spot the difference' routine, with the biblical narration on one side of the page and the school nativity on the other. The shepherds and magi shouldn't be on the stage at the same time; neither Matthew or Luke mentions a donkey; Mary's clothing would have been far from spotless.

I wonder why we do that? Perhaps we think if we focus on the idea that the magi didn't make it to the manger, or indeed the fact that Matthew makes no mention of a manger in the first place, we can avoid the uncomfortable truths in the story.

In true Jesus fashion, even the events of his early days are, let's say, a tad controversial. Whether we know them as 'Kings', 'Magi' or 'Wise Men' two facts remain: they were particularly accomplished in astrology which was a highly regarded science in those days; and they were not Jews but followers of an eastern religion, probably Zoroastrianism.

God uses their faith and knowledge to bring them to Christ. More than that, God used them to let King Herod and the chief priests and scribes of the people in on the news that their Messiah had been born.

Historical accuracy aside, if that doesn't earn them a place in the nativity scene I'm not sure what will.

What can you learn from those who do not share your beliefs?

NEW YEAR'S DAY
Read Matthew 2: 7-11

The gifts of the magi were opulent and exciting.

Gold had long been the extravagant gift of choice. Might it represent the richness of Jesus' kingship?

In Old Testament times frankincense featured in worship – carrying prayers from earth to heaven. Does its presence reflect Jesus' divinity?

Myrrh had been used to anoint and purify the dead for many centuries. Is it intended to indicate the apparent brevity of Jesus' earthly life?

Whatever hidden meanings we might ascribe we must remember this: the magi were strangers from a distant land who knew nothing of the Messiah or the prophecies surrounding him. They didn't know where this story was going. They saw a light in the sky, realised it foreshadowed a king, and gathered together what seemed appropriate gifts, the relevance of which only became clear later.

The magi's situation is unique, but can you see echoes in your life:

Seemingly innocous decisions that changed the course of a life?

Gifts whose importance you only recognised afterward?

Realising you have just had a profound experience of God?

So we join the magi in kneeling at Jesus' feet and place our gifts – some plain for all to see and others known only to God – alongside theirs. We do not know where this story is going or what significance they may have. Those things are in God's hands.

Story

What gifts do you bring before God?

Thank you

Wisdom

2ND JANUARY
Read Matthew 2: 12-13

What's your favourite film?

Mine varies from day to day but usually resides in the fantasy / sci-fi category. There's something strangely comfortable about recognising familiar emotions, concepts and struggles under the thin veil of another world or time.

When a plot is complex or has more than one storyline its common to include some sort of exposition scene where the characters sum up all that has already happened and offer key pieces of information about what is to come. If done well the viewer will not realise the importance of this sequence until later, if at all.

The incarnation is full of moments like this. The Great Director steps in with a dream or vision which offers vital insight and enables the story to continue. They occur with such regularity we might fail to notice them, especially if we're familiar with how things unfold.

'This is what's really going on,' God whispers into the dreams of Joseph and the magi, 'and this is what you must do in response.'

Thus the magi delay Herod and his army just long enough for Joseph to flee the country with Mary and the baby.

There is little point in speculating what would have happened had these dreams not taken place or been ignored. However, we may well question how often we disregard The Great Director's endeavours to speak into our own lives.

Are you sometimes stumped by developments in your own storyline? Do you need to ask God for some form of exposition scene?

Prayer is not just 'talking to God'. Prayer is a conversation.

3RD JANUARY
Read Matthew 2: 14-15

With a gasp, Joseph awakes from an anxious, fitful sleep and instinctively he glances at the mother and child still peaceful at his side. He offers a quick but heartfelt mutter of thanksgiving.

It wasn't just another nightmare, he's sure. After all, it isn't the first time he's received unlikely news from an equally improbable source. He looks again at Mary and the baby. He made a promise to God the day the angel came. He'll fulfil his commitment now.

Shaking away sleep he begins to gather their possessions. Let them rest. It might be a while before they'll lie down in comfort again.

Finally there's nothing for it. "Mary."

In past months he's wondered at her ability to go from fast asleep to wide awake in a moment, often pre-empting Jesus' cries.

She doesn't fail him now. Her eyes open and instantly meet his.

'I've had a dream,' he said. 'We have to run.' Once those words would have sounded comical, his urgency ridiculous, but she merely nods, scoops up Jesus, blankets and all, and comes to his side.

'Where?'

'Egypt. He'll be safe.' His thumb finds Jesus' cheek. This is life now.

Two-thousand years later there are still those who fear for their lives; who cannot unpack and declare a place 'home'; who are forced to become dependent on the kindness of strangers.

Would you have welcomed them; or told them to 'go home'?

Imagine you were native to the Egyptian town in which Mary, Joseph and Jesus settled.

How would you behave towards them?

4TH JANUARY
Read Matthew 2: 16

One verse. Just one. Hidden away in a part of Matthew's gospel many would consider best avoided.

Is the 'slaughter of the innocents' a historical fact? Probably not. Is it vital to our understanding of Jesus' life and ministry? Absolutely.

Matthew uses Herod as an example of kingship gone wrong. This isn't entirely without cause; he was certainly a despot and responsible for killing at least two of his own sons. This king believes he has the right to rule and can dispose of anyone in his way. His voice drips with power. One word from him and all hell breaks lose.

What happens to such a person when their power is threatened? A brief glance at the history books tells us the answer. Ordinary people suffer. Children are cut down before their lives take root.

Herod was the king, but he was also a convert to Judaism. He'd heard the prophecies. The coming Messiah would tear up Herod's hierarchy and knit together the oppressed. Surely he would have felt threatened by the news the Wise Men brought with them.

The Messiah-king breaking into the world would be a sharp contrast to Herod. This king came not to be served but to serve, and teaches his ways to anyone wishing to learn. His voice drips with power. One word from him and the sick are healed, the stumbling are caught and the struggling find new meaning to their lives.

Herod is remembered as a destroyer of innocents. Jesus as a defender of the weak.

How do you use the power you hold over others?

Pray for those with power over others and those suffering due to misuse of power.

5TH JANUARY
Read Matthew 2: 16-18

These verses contain so much that is heartbreakingly familiar to so many, it seems almost churlish to explore any further.

This is no place for platitudes. You almost certainly know at least one person whose child has died, before or after birth, even if you do not know their story. Perhaps you have supported a friend or family member through bereavement. It may have been your child who died. If so, continue carefully and remember you are held in prayer by me as I write, and by all who read today's reflection.

Matthew 2: 16-18 presents the worst of human experience. Attempting to make sense of this gets us no-where. So we sit with those affected by child-loss and know that others sit with us:

Any who mourn a life that never got to be lived.

Any who didn't get to bring the baby home.

Any whose child died unexpectedly or suddenly.

Any who spent months or years next to hospital beds.

Any who still recall the knock at the door.

Any who already dread next Christmas.

Any for whom these verses evoke painful memories.

Sometimes there are no 'right words'. Sometimes we can only be present to one another; holding each other before God and sharing space.

Remember those lives cut short, and those they left behind.

Hold anyone affected by child-bereavement before God in prayer.

THE EPIPHANY
Read: Matthew 2 and Luke 2

Take a glance back at the 'Day 1' reflection on John 1: 1-14.

Throughout Advent we hear of God's impact on a specific, though unlikely, group of people, culminating in the incarnation. At Epiphany we celebrate Jesus reaching beyond his immediate circle to offer the same new life to all those who recognised him as something special, whoever they might be.

At Advent and Christmas we hear a familiar story. At Epiphany we witness earth and heaven, all roaring 'Look! This is why it matters!' Jesus' story isn't just for specific people in the first-century AD, but for todays:

Zechariahs; who have doubts.
Elizabeths: who are scorned and shamed.
Johns: who may not see the fruits of their labour.
Marys: who follow God's call even when the way isn't obvious or easy.
Josephs: who look so ordinary and yet carry the world in their arms.
Non-nuclear family: who value love over blood.
Vulnerable people: who can count Jesus among their number.
Manual workers: whose true value is known to God.
Magi: who speak other languages and find God in different places.
Simeons: drawn to speak uncomfortable or painful truths.
Annas: who know how to hold space and have wisdom to spare.
Leaders of the nations: whose actions have consequences.
Rachels: with whom God weeps.
You and me: even when we don't know how or why.

If you ask me, that's the miracle; the 'reason for the season'; the cause for celebration not just for a few weeks per year but always.

What are the most important
lessons you've learned since
the beginning of Advent?

How can you carry them
through into this year?

REVISITING

THE

OLD

Reflections on the Old Testament

Coming Soon!
The next in the series.

BY DEACON LAURA EVANS